The Quotation Bank for A-Level

Othello

William Shakespeare

Copyright © 2022 Esse Publishing Limited and Amy Smith
The moral rights of the authors have been asserted.

First published in 2022 by:
The Quotation Bank
Esse Publishing Limited
10 9 8 7 6 5 4 3 2 1

All rights reserved. No part of this publication may be reproduced, resold, stored in a retrieval system or transmitted in any form, or by any means (electronic, photocopying, mechanical or otherwise) without the prior written permission of both the copyright owners and the publisher.

A CIP catalogue record for this book is available from the British Library.
ISBN 978-1-9999816-5-5

All enquiries to: contact@thequotationbank.co.uk
Every effort has been made to trace and contact all relevant copyright holders. However, if contacted the publisher will rectify any omission or error at the earliest opportunity.

Printed and bound by Target Print Limited, Broad Lane, Cottenham, Cambridge CB24 8SW.

www.thequotationbank.co.uk

Introduction

How The Quotation Bank can help you in your exams	4
How to use The Quotation Bank	5

Quotations

Act One	6
Act Two	12
Act Three	19
Act Four	23
Act Five	26
Critical and Contextual Quotations	31

Revision and Essay Planning

Performance History	41
How to revise effectively	42
Suggested revision activities	43
Glossary	44

Welcome to The Quotation Bank, the comprehensive guide to all the key quotations you need to succeed in your exams.

Whilst you may have read the play, watched a film adaptation, understood the plot and have a strong grasp of context, all questions in your A-Levels require you to write a focused essay, full of textual references and quotations (be they textual, critical or contextual), and most importantly, quotations that you then analyse.

I think we all agree it is **analysis** that is the tricky part – and that is why we are here to help!

The Quotation Bank takes 25 of the most important quotations from the text, interprets them, analyses them, highlights literary techniques Shakespeare has used, puts them in context, and suggests which quotations you might use in which essays. We have also included 10 contextual and critical quotations, analysed them, and linked them closely to the text, all for you to explore.

At the end of **The Quotation Bank** we have put together a performance history and great revision exercises to help you prepare for your exam. We have also included a detailed glossary to make sure you completely understand what certain literary terms actually mean!

How The Quotation Bank can help you in your exams.

The Quotation Bank is designed to make sure every point you make in an essay clearly fulfils the Assessment Objectives an examiner will be using when marking your work.

Every quotation comes with the following detailed material:

Interpretation: The interpretation of each quotation allows you to fulfil **AO1**, articulating an informed, personal response, and **AO5**, using different interpretations to inform your exploration of the text.

Techniques: Using associated concepts and terminology (in this case, the techniques used by Shakespeare) is a key part of **AO1**, and can help you identify and analyse ways in which meanings are shaped (**AO2**).

Analysis: We have provided as much analysis (**AO2**) as possible, as well as exploring the significance and influence of contextual material (**AO3**) and different interpretations (**AO5**). It is a great idea to analyse the quotation in detail – you need to do more than just say what it means, but also try to explore a variety of different ways of interpreting it.

Use in essays on… Your answer needs to be focused to fulfil **AO1**. This section helps you choose relevant quotations and link them together for a stronger, more detailed essay.

How to use The Quotation Bank.

Many students spend time learning quotations by heart. This can be useful, but it is important to remember what you are meant to do with quotations once you get into the exam.

By using **The Quotation Bank**, not only will you have a huge number of textual, critical and contextual quotations to use in your essays, you will also have ideas on what to say about them, how to analyse them, how to link them together, and what questions to use them for.

These quotations can form the basis of your answer, making sure every point **articulates an informed, personal response (AO1)** and allows you to **analyse ways in which meanings are shaped (AO2)**.

The critical and contextual quotations allow you to easily and effectively explore the significance and influence of **context (AO3)**, and provide you with a variety of **different readings to explore (AO5).**

The textual quotations cover the whole text to allow you to show comprehensive whole text knowledge, and the critical and contextual quotations cover the full range of the text's publication history to help you explore the contexts in which the text was both **written and received (AO3)**.

Act One Scene One:

IAGO: "I am not what I am."

Interpretation: Iago informs Roderigo that he adopts a façade, hiding his true self and pretending loyalty to Othello. Shakespeare clearly reveals Iago's deceptive nature.

Techniques: Allusion; Repetition; Present Tense.

Analysis:
- The Biblical allusion is to Exodus 3:14, in which God reveals his eternal, unchanging goodness in the statement "I am who I am". Shakespeare's inversion of this phrase indicates Iago's devilish and "Janus-faced" nature.
- The present tense hints that, paradoxically, Iago's protean nature is unchanging.
- It is structurally important that the audience encounters the tragic villain before the tragic hero, and that Iago's dual nature is quickly revealed to the audience. Shakespeare develops a sense of complicity with Iago's charismatic character, prompting the audience to consider how their sympathy for such a heinous villain may reveal their own base instincts.

Use in essays on… The Tragic Villain; Appearance and Reality; Deception and Treachery.

Act One Scene One:
IAGO: "Even now, now, very now, an old black ram/Is tupping your white ewe."

Interpretation: Iago's racism reveals engrained prejudices, and Shakespeare uses this to highlight the external pressures society places upon the tragic hero.

Techniques: Repetition; Imagery; Juxtaposition.

Analysis:
- The repetition and present tense create a sense of urgency, demonstrating Iago's manipulative skill as he rouses Brabantio to immediate action.
- The animal imagery exemplifies the racist stereotypes which surround Othello, presenting him as debased, sexualised, and uncivilised. It is important that Othello has not yet appeared on stage, as Shakespeare creates an impression of the tragic hero which will be debunked at the start of Act One Scene Two.
- Whilst the juxtaposition of colours exposes Iago's obsession with ethnicity, the use of animal imagery for both lovers also reflects his misogyny. Desdemona is objectified and rendered passive.

Use in essays on… Race; The Tragic Villain; The Tragic Hero; Gender.

Act One Scene Two:
OTHELLO: "My services which I have done the signiory / Shall out-tongue his complaints."

Interpretation: In contrast to the debased descriptions of Othello in Act One Scene One, here Shakespeare presents him as rational, calm, and noble. However, arguably Othello's self-confidence suggests hubris and a misunderstanding of his role within Venetian society; after all, he is a hired mercenary, not a member of the ruling elite.

Techniques: Blank Verse; Modal Verb; Motif.

Analysis:
- The blank verse contrasts with Iago's descent into prose in Act One Scene One: the former represents order and rationality, whilst the latter indicates chaos.
- The modal verb "shall" clearly conveys Othello's confidence that he will prevail. Is this suggestive of a level of hubris?
- Throughout the play, the motif of storytelling suggests that the individual who controls the narrative can wield power. Here, this is shown in Othello's belief that his story will "out-tongue" Brabantio's version of events.

Use in essays on… The Tragic Hero; Race; Rationality vs Irrationality.

Act One Scene Three:
DESDEMONA: "[I]f I be left behind, / A moth of peace, and he go to the war, / The rites for which I love him are bereft me."

Interpretation: By bringing Desdemona on stage to articulate her wishes before the senators, Shakespeare emphasises her confidence and commitment to Othello. However, she has been given permission to speak: the seeds of Othello's control are being sown.

Techniques: Staging; Imagery.

Analysis:
- The staging emblematises the blending of public and private concerns, as Desdemona speaks in a political, masculine space, and the Duke's acceptance of the marriage is influenced by the need to send Othello to war. We see how private lives can be determined by public events, and can also consider how a leader's personal situation may potentially destabilise the public realm.
- The word "moth" means idler, suggesting that whilst men occupy the sphere of action, women are consigned to boredom in the domestic sphere.

Use in essays on… The Tragic Victim; Gender; Personal and Political Spheres.

Act One Scene Three:
> **BRABANTIO: "Look to her, Moor, if thou hast eyes to see: / She has deceived her father, and may thee."**

Interpretation: Whilst it is Iago who stokes the fires of Othello's jealousy, it is actually Brabantio who originally mentions betrayal. In this quotation we see the influence of medieval morality plays on the tragedy, with the message being to avoid making an unequal matrimonial match.

Techniques: Imagery; Rhyming Couplet.

Analysis:
- Imagery of sight is a motif throughout the play, and here Shakespeare emphasises the characters' dependence on visible evidence.
- The rhyming couplet indicates the finality and almost prophetic quality of Brabantio's words. It is important to note that Iago is present on stage as a silent spectator, and he echoes Brabantio's words in Act Three Scene Three ("She did deceive her father, marrying you").

Use in essays on… Love and Marriage; Jealousy; Appearance and Reality.

Act One Scene Three:
IAGO: "Virtue? A fig! 'Tis in ourselves that we are thus or thus. Our bodies are our gardens, to the which our souls are gardeners."

Interpretation: In contrast to the nobility and honesty demonstrated by the new couple earlier in the scene, here Shakespeare emphasises Iago's debasement. Iago manipulates Biblical imagery as he says that man has control over his own existence and character.

Techniques: Prose; Allusion; Pronouns.

Analysis:
- The use of prose creates a sense of chaos, contrasting sharply with the preceding conversation between Othello, Desdemona, and the senators.
- The Biblical Parable of the Sower (Mark 4) presents God as a gardener; here, Iago challenges this idea, insisting that he has free will to determine his own existence. This echoes the contemporary debate between fate and free will.
- The pronoun "our" includes Roderigo, but it also stretches out to include the audience, developing complicity with the tragic villain.

Use in essays on... The Tragic Villain; Fate vs Free Will; Debasement.

Act Two Scene One:
 IAGO: "[T]o diet my revenge, / For that I do suspect the lusty Moor / Hath leap'd into my seat, the thought whereof / Doth like a poisonous mineral gnaw my inwards."

Interpretation: Whereas Iago's character may be used for comic effect in Act One, here his villainy is foregrounded; Shakespeare emphasises his vengeful attitude, suggesting that one of his motivations is sexual jealousy – a weapon which Iago will turn against Othello.

Techniques: Imagery; Euphemism.

Analysis:
- Imagery of food is used to communicate Iago's insatiable desire for vengeance.
- Imagery of poison is used to convey the unstoppable power of jealousy once it has taken hold. Shakespeare suggests that this emotion has a visceral impact, as Iago experiences extreme, continual pain ("gnaw").
- The euphemism "leap'd into my seat" suggests that Iago believes Othello has had an affair with Emilia; Shakespeare indicates Iago's misogynistic desire to control his wife's body.

Use in essays on… The Tragic Villain; Gender; Jealousy.

Act Two Scene Three:
OTHELLO: "My blood begins my safer guides to rule, / And passion having my best judgement collied, / Assays to lead the way."

Interpretation: This is the play's key turning point: Othello transforms from rational to irrational. There is much debate about whether Shakespeare confirms racial stereotypes, or if he is exploring the impact of external pressures on the human mind.

Techniques: Juxtaposition; Imagery; Motif.

Analysis:
- Throughout the play, the motif of "judgement" is associated with reason and is the hallmark of a successful leader. "Passion" is linked with personal emotion and suggests that a leader is losing perspective.
- The imagery of "rul[ing]" connects the personal and political. As in many of Shakespeare's plays, as leaders become unable to rule their own minds, so too are they unable to rule the state.

Use in essays on… The Tragic Hero; Leadership; Rationality vs Irrationality; Personal and Political Spheres.

Act Two Scene Three:
> **OTHELLO: "All's well now sweeting; come away to bed."**

Interpretation: As well as marking a turning point in Othello's leadership, Act Two Scene Three marks a shift in his marriage; ostensible equality gives way to Othello's overt dominance, and Desdemona becomes increasingly consigned to the domestic sphere.

Techniques: Language; Imperative; Staging.

Analysis:
- Shakespeare uses the diminutive term "sweeting" to contrast with the earlier "my fair warrior", revealing how patriarchal ideas – which were implicit within the marriage in Act One – have now become prevalent in the relationship.
- By using the imperative verb "come", Shakespeare cements Othello's control within the marriage.
- Whereas Desdemona was invited to speak in front of the senators in Act One, here she appears only fleetingly and is given few lines; her public role has diminished and she is increasingly marginalised.

Use in essays on… The Tragic Hero; The Tragic Victim; Gender.

Act Two Scene Three:
CASSIO: "Reputation, reputation, reputation! O, I have lost my reputation! I have lost the immortal part of myself, and what remains is bestial."

Interpretation: Cassio's disintegration foreshadows Othello's later transformation, and allows Shakespeare to pose the play's central question: what does it mean to be human?

Techniques: Prose; Repetition; Juxtaposition.

Analysis:
- Shakespeare uses prose and repetition to signal the shift from order to chaos.
- The juxtaposition of "immortal"/"bestial" echoes other dichotomies: judgement/passion, rational/irrational. Cassio believes his debauchery leads to a loss of his identity, his social position, and his salvation.
- The echo of the animalistic language used elsewhere to describe Othello gives weight to the argument that Shakespeare is more interested in the human condition than the concept of race – regardless of ethnicity, several of the play's characters reflect on the debasement of their souls.

Use in essays on… Rationality vs Irrationality; Debasement.

Act Two Scene Three:
IAGO: "So will I turn her virtue into pitch, / And out of her own goodness make the net / That shall enmesh them all."

Interpretation: Shakespeare continues to emphasise Iago's vengeful villainy and his manipulative character, as he seeks to pervert all that is good in his quest for control.

Techniques: Soliloquy; Modal Verb; Imagery.

Analysis:
- Unusually, Shakespeare gives the tragic villain more soliloquies than the hero, building the audience's sense of complicity with Iago rather than with Othello.
- The modal verb "will" not only articulates Iago's determination, but also his hubristic certainty that he will prevail.
- The image of the "net" echoes that of the spider's web used earlier in the play. Shakespeare reveals that Iago does not simply desire destruction: he desires control and ascendency in order to compensate for his feeling of inferiority.

Use in essays on… The Tragic Villain; The Tragic Victim; Appearance and Reality.

Act Three Scene Three:
  OTHELLO: "I do love thee; and when I love thee not, / Chaos is come again."

Interpretation: Shakespeare presents Othello oscillating between love and hatred for Desdemona, raising a key question in the play: is Othello responsible for his own actions, or is Iago a necessary catalyst, without whom the murder would not have happened?

Techniques: Motif; Imagery; Present Tense.

Analysis:
- These lines echo Othello's passionate statement of love earlier in the play: "I love the gentle Desdemona". Yet here, the profession of love is coupled not just with doubt, but also with the certainty that there will be occasions of indifference – expressed in the adverb "when".
- Shakespeare connects a lack of love with the image of chaos, which is both psychological (epitomised in Othello's later fit), and public (as violence increases in the public sphere). In doing so, Shakespeare is exploring the importance of the leader's psychological wellbeing on the governance of the state.

Use in essays on... The Tragic Hero; Love and Marriage; Leadership; Personal and Political Spheres.

Act Three Scene Three:
 OTHELLO: "Think, my lord! By heaven, he echoes me, / As if there were some monster in his thought / Too hideous to be shown."

Interpretation: Shakespeare demonstrates the methodology of an experienced manipulator, as Iago plants the seeds of doubt and jealousy in Othello's mind. One is struck by the frailty of the human mind to external forces.

Techniques: Repetition; Imagery.

Analysis:
- The rapid repetition of "think" in this scene – which culminates in this statement by Othello – reveals how Iago plays on Othello's vulnerable mind, and allows Shakespeare to create an urgent pace, as the play accelerates towards its (almost) inevitable conclusion.
- As shown in Othello's speech in Act One Scene Three, monsters enter the early modern imagination from distant lands, presenting a challenge to order and peace. Here, the image represents the disruption jealousy causes to the mind.

Use in essays on... The Tragic Hero; The Tragic Villain; Rationality vs Irrationality; Jealousy.

Act Three Scene Three:
OTHELLO: "Damn her, lewd minx! O, damn her, damn her!"

Interpretation: Shakespeare presents Othello's continued decline into violence and debasement. In the play's double-time scheme, this could happen in a matter of days, or across a longer time span.

Techniques: Imagery; Language.

Analysis:
- A process of linguistic convergence had led Othello to adopt the profanities which were previously common in Iago's speech. This emphasises the change from Othello's eloquent, restrained speeches in Act One.
- Whereas animal imagery was applied to Othello in Act One, he now applies it to Desdemona. Yet, more commonly "minx" signified a wanton woman – a meaning reinforced through the adjective "lewd". Whilst the play's exposition highlighted the couple's emotional connection ("soul"), Shakespeare is now indicating that Othello has become debased by poisonous sexual jealousy.

Use in essays on… The Tragic Hero; The Tragic Victim; Rationality vs Irrationality; Jealousy.

Act Three Scene Four:
> **EMILIA: "They are all but stomachs, and we all but food; / They eat us hungerly, and when they are full, / They belch us."**

Interpretation: As Shakespeare presents Desdemona's descent from outspoken to passive, so too does he dramatize Emilia's increasing confidence. She becomes a proto-feminist voice, arguing against the exploitation of women.

Techniques: Imagery; Pronouns.

Analysis:
- Whilst Emilia's use of food imagery echoes Iago's, she uses it to express her frustration at the sexual exploitation of women. Her words articulate a dissatisfaction with the debasement of love to a dismissive "belch".
- The use of the divisive pronouns "they" and "we" indicates an almost insuperable separation between the genders; the dramatic action of the play seems to confirm this, as the central couple are propelled from ostensible equality and union to death on the symbolic marriage bed.

Use in essays on... Gender; Jealousy; Debasement; Love and Marriage.

Act Four Scene One:
OTHELLO: "Is't possible? – Confess? Handkerchief? O devil!" [*He falls into a trance.*]

Interpretation: Shakespeare dramatizes the continued disintegration of Othello's mind, until the noble hero is seen lying in a fit at the feet of the tragic villain.

Techniques: Sentence Structure; Motif; Staging.

Analysis:
- Othello's psychological collapse is reflected in the disintegration of his language; his previous eloquence declines into prose comprised of sentence fragments, half-questions, repeated phrases, and – eventually – silence.
- The repetition of "handkerchief" throughout Act Three indicates Othello's obsession with this piece of "ocular proof" – whilst the handkerchief certainly symbolises Desdemona's body, it may also signify her chastity or infidelity, her marriage vows and wedding sheets, or her betrayal.
- The staging of this scene is powerful, as a black man lies incapacitated at the feet of a white villain, allowing Shakespeare to heighten pathos for Othello.

Use in essays on… Race; The Tragic Hero; The Tragic Villain; Jealousy.

Act Four Scene One:
> **LODOVICO: "Is this the noble Moor whom our full senate / Call all-in-all sufficient? Is this the nature / Whom passion could not shake?"**

Interpretation: Shakespeare uses Lodovico as a commentator on the action. Absent for the whole of Act Two, he arrives after Othello's mind starts to disintegrate, and can therefore draw the audience's attention to the differences he sees in the General.

Techniques: Motif; Juxtaposition; Rhetorical Questions; Adjective.

Analysis:
- The use of rhetorical questions suggests Lodovico's complete confusion at the situation he finds in Cyprus.
- The motif of passion/reason recurs here, as Lodovico believes Othello has declined from noble to irrational.
- The adjectives "noble" and "sufficient" indicate the high esteem and status Othello has previously enjoyed, reminding the audience of the great heights from which Othello has quickly fallen.

Use in essays on… Leadership; The Tragic Hero; Rationality vs Irrationality.

Act Four Scene Two:
OTHELLO: "I took you for that cunning whore of Venice / That married with Othello."

Interpretation: Othello refers to English stereotypes of Venetian women, judging Desdemona by the licentious culture associated with her home city.

Techniques: Language; Third Person; Tone.

Analysis:

- Shakespeare's use of sexually debased language reveals the transformation of Othello from a noble, chivalrous husband to one obsessed with sexual transgression. Othello's readiness to judge Desdemona based on stereotypes sits uneasily, as the tragic hero has been subject to such harsh treatment elsewhere in the play.
- The use of the third person indicates a recurrence of the storytelling motif; Othello narrates his life in Act One Scene Three, and again in Act Five Scene One. This suggests a level of detachment from Desdemona.

Use in essays on… The Tragic Hero; The Tragic Victim; Rationality vs Irrationality.

Act Five Scene Two:
DESDEMONA: "Some bloody passion shakes your very frame."

Interpretation: Shakespeare frames the murder of Desdemona in terms of the recurring dichotomy of passion and reason. At this intensely emotional moment, Desdemona recognises that her husband is consumed by irrational violence.

Techniques: Imagery; Motif; Staging.

Analysis:
- The word "blood" is used throughout the play to signify both violent acts and a loss of control. Here, Othello's "blood" is truly "rul[ing]" "his safer guides" (see Act Two Scene Three), propelling the couple to their inevitable denouement.
- Whereas so many of the play's earlier scenes have occurred in public and political spaces, this final scene is staged in the couple's private bedchamber, with the white wedding sheets placed on the bed. It is ironic that in this intimate setting, the tragic hero's "passion" propels him to murder rather than to consummate his marriage vows.

Use in essays on… Love and Marriage; Jealousy; The Tragic Hero; The Tragic Victim.

Act Five Scene Two:
 DESDEMONA: "Nobody; I myself. Farewell. / Commend me to my kind lord."

Interpretation: Shakespeare emphasises Desdemona's love and complete submission to Othello, as she claims that she has caused her own death. Some modern interpretations explore this from the perspective of coercive control and domestic violence.

Techniques: Language; Pronouns; Dramatic Device; Tone.

Analysis:
- The submissive language, unfailing reverence for the murderous Othello, and the calm, accepting tone highlights Desdemona's continuing love.
- The possessive pronoun "my" indicates the love which Desdemona believes still binds her to her husband.
- This occurrence is extremely surprising, as Desdemona is temporarily resurrected to attest to Othello's innocence. As a dramatic device, it heightens our pathos for Desdemona and extenuates hope for her survival, thus intensifying the sorrow at her eventual death.

Use in essays on… The Tragic Victim; Love and Marriage; Gender.

Act Five Scene Two:
EMILIA: "I will speak as liberal as the north."

Interpretation: As Desdemona becomes increasingly subservient and is violently silenced, Emilia finds her voice. Is Shakespeare using Emilia to articulate the injustices wrought by patriarchal societies? Or does the subsequent silencing of Emilia indicate that women cannot attain power?

Techniques: Staging; Verb Usage; Imagery.

Analysis:
- This scene parallels Act One Scene Three, as here we see a woman speaking her mind in front of a group of political leaders. However, where Desdemona was invited to speak, here Emilia finds her voice despite the threat of violence. This context emphasises Emilia's newfound determination and strength.
- The modal verb "will" (often used by Iago) communicates Emilia's resolve.
- The "north" refers to the bitterly cold north wind, a natural image which may indicate the correctness of Emilia's actions.

Use in essays on... Gender; Personal and Political Spheres; Power.

Act Five Scene Two:
IAGO: "Demand me nothing; what you know, you know. / From this time forth I never will speak word."

Interpretation: Iago's final words have frustrated audiences for centuries, as the question of his motivation and ultimate ambition is left unanswered. It is also notable that, unusually, the tragic villain survives the play, symbolically suggesting that evil has not been (or cannot be) completely vanquished.

Techniques: Imperative; Modal Verb; Motif.

Analysis:
- Shakespeare continues to highlight Iago's control through the use of the imperative verb; he retains power even as he is led off to be tortured.
- The modal verb "will" indicates Iago's certainty.
- Throughout the play, the character who controls the narrative and speaks most persuasively has gained ascendency. However, here power lies in the refusal to speak.

Use in essays on... The Tragic Villain; Power.

Act Five Scene Two:
OTHELLO: "Then must you speak / Of one that lov'd not wisely, but too well; / Of one not easily jealous but, being wrought, / Perplex'd in the extreme."

Interpretation: The storytelling motif continues in Othello's final speech, as he constructs a narrative of his life. However, the inaccuracies of this tale lead the audience to question whether the tragic hero achieves anagnorisis. Whereas the adage "know thyself" is the foundation of the tragic genre, Othello dies without self-understanding.

Techniques: Motif; Third Person.

Analysis:
- The use of the third person indicates that Othello is stepping outside himself to weave his own history; does this indicate an avoidance of responsibility?
- The word "wisely" means moderately, suggesting that Othello believes he loved Desdemona too passionately.
- Othello's claim that he is "not easily jealous" is highly doubtful, as he believed in Desdemona's guilt after only a few hints from Iago.

Use in essays on… The Tragic Hero; Jealousy; Appearance and Reality.

Samuel Johnson (1765) argues that,
"Though it will perhaps not be said of him as he says of himself, that he is 'a man not easily jealous', yet we cannot but pity him when at last we find him 'perplexed in the extreme.'"

Interpretation: Although Johnson doubts Othello's self-understanding, he is more sympathetic than earlier critics, such as Thomas Rymer, who dismiss the play as absurd. Johnson feels pathos for Othello as his jealousy has been elicited by Iago's manipulation.

Analysis:
- Our pathos for Othello depends on how we interpret Iago's control. Iago's soliloquies and the dialogue with Othello in Act Three Scene Three demonstrate his power over others, as he weaves the "net / That shall enmesh them all".
- However, it could be argued that Othello is not as passive as suggested by the phrase "perplexed in the extreme". Shakespeare uses the double time-scheme to convey the speed at which Othello's jealousy grows, and in his final dialogue with Desdemona he hears her protestations of innocence. In this light, it is Othello himself who makes a free decision to commit murder.

Use in essays on... The Tragic Hero; The Tragic Villain; Fate vs Free Will; Deception and Treachery.

S.T. Coleridge (1819) describes,
   "**The motive-hunting of motiveless malignity – how awful! In itself fiendish.**"

Interpretation: Coleridge focusses on Iago, concluding there is little evidence that his evil nature has a specific cause. This interpretation sees Iago as a devilish character who takes an aesthetic pleasure in destruction.

Analysis:
- There are various potential motivations for Iago's actions, from his frustrated desire for promotion, jealousy of a sexual relationship between Othello and Emilia, and "lust" for Desdemona. Some critics interpret the quasi-marriage scene at the conclusion of Act Three Scene Three as evidence of Iago's unrequited erotic desire for Othello.
- Arguably, the most likely explanation for Iago's actions is "motiveless" revulsion against morality and goodness. Speaking of Cassio, Iago admits "He hath a daily beauty in his life / That makes me ugly" (Act Five Scene One).
- Ultimately, Iago's silence at the denouement denies any resolution to this topic.

Use in essays on… The Tragic Villain; Deception and Treachery; Debasement.

A.C Bradley (1904) suggests,
> "But Iago, finally, is not simply a man of action; he is an artist. His action is a plot, an intricate plot of a drama, and in the conception and execution of it he experiences the tension and the joy of artistic creation."

Interpretation: Bradley comments on Iago's control and power, comparing it to that of an author creating a text. Like Coleridge, Bradley sees that Iago's true motivation is the pleasure he takes in being a puppeteer, using his deep knowledge of human nature to elicit particular responses and actions from others.

Analysis:
- Shakespeare uses Iago's soliloquies to demonstrate the aesthetic pleasure he takes in plotting – see the end of Act One Scene Three and Act Two Scene Three.
- Shakespeare also indicates that, outside of the battlefield, Iago generally shies away from physical action, preferring to manipulate others to commit his desired deeds. For example, at the start of Act Five Scene One, Iago watches while Roderigo is sent forward to stab Cassio.

Use in essays on… The Tragic Villain; Deception and Treachery; Debasement; Power.

A.C. Bradley (1904) asserts that,
> "Such jealousy as Othello's converts human nature into chaos, and liberates the beast in man."

Interpretation: Bradley distinguishes *Othello* from Shakespearean plays which focus on the political ambitions of the tragic hero; he sees this text as being about sexual jealousy. As such, Bradley believes *Othello* depicts a greater intensity of suffering.

Analysis:
- Shakespeare explores the dichotomies of human/beast, rational/irrational, reason/passion. As passion dominates, Othello is increasingly violent, and his language is more debased (animalistic imagery, prose, sentence fragments).
- Shakespeare considers the impact that a leader's personal chaos may have on the public sphere – and so we see violence spreading in Act Two Scene Three and Act Five Scene One, threatening to destabilise the inner workings of a crucial military outpost which secures Europe's safety.
- However, Othello's soliloquy in Act Five Scene One is chilling in its coldness. It seems that Othello acts not from animal instinct, but from misguided reason.

Use in essays on… The Tragic Hero; Debasement; Jealousy; Personal and Political Spheres.

F.R. Leavis (1952) states,
> "Iago is subordinate and merely ancillary. He is not much more than a necessary piece of dramatic mechanism."

Interpretation: Unlike many other critics (such as Coleridge), Leavis sees Othello as being the central character in this play. Leavis describes Iago as being a dramatic device who is brought to life on stage in order to prompt Othello's downfall.

Analysis:
- Arguably, Iago is a mere catalyst for Othello's actions. He prompts Roderigo to awaken Brabantio, watches while Othello defends himself to the senators, toys with the handkerchief, and stage-manages various conversations.
- However, it is more convincing that Shakespeare was using Iago to explore the themes of deception and evil. Whereas the tragic hero has a limited number of asides and soliloquies, the charismatic tragic villain is given several key speeches in which Shakespeare builds his complicity with the audience. It is also Iago's refusal to explain his deeds which most fascinates the audience after the play's conclusion.

Use in essays on… The Tragic Villain; The Tragic Hero; Deception and Treachery.

G.K. Hunter (1967) contends that,
"The dark reality originating in Iago's soul spreads across the play, blackening whatever it overcomes and making the deeds of Othello at last fit in with the prejudice that his face at first excited."

Interpretation: From the mid-twentieth century, critics were increasingly interested in the play's racial and gender politics. Here, Hunter argues that Iago shapes Othello into a racist stereotype – rather than Othello's noble identity being a veneer hiding innate irrational rage and barely controlled emotions.

Analysis:
- This interpretation can be supported by the images of poison, disease, and control which are used throughout the text ("poison his delight", "plague him with flies" and "the Moor already changes with my poison").
- Shakespeare emphasises both Iago's racist prejudices ("black ram") and Othello's nobility from the outset. Hunter believes that Othello's change is not a revelation of his "true" nature, but due to Iago's influence. This is suggested when Othello descends into irrational rage, as his words echo Iago's.

Use in essays on… The Tragic Hero; The Tragic Villain; Deception and Treachery; Debasement.

Marilyn French (1982) insists Desdemona,
   "accepts her culture's dictum that she must be obedient to males".

Interpretation: French is interested in the patriarchal and misogynistic ideologies which operate in the play, and she argues that Desdemona is ultimately subservient and submissive to this culture.

Analysis:
- As the play progresses, Shakespeare increasingly emphasises Desdemona's submissive character – and this is particularly revealed in the "willow scene" (in which Desdemona seems to be aware that she is proceeding towards her death) and in her temporary resurrection in Act Five Scene Two.
- However, arguably Desdemona does not accept "her culture's dictum" at the start of the play, as she speaks confidently in front of the senators and insists that she will not remain "a moth of peace". Despite this, Desdemona is given male permission to speak in this context, and is seeking permission to travel with her husband; this does suggest that the seeds of subservience are sown early on.

Use in essays on… The Tragic Victim; Gender; Love and Marriage.

Karen Newman (1991) declares,
> "Shakespeare's play stands in contestatory relation to the hegemonic ideologies of race and gender in early modern England."

Interpretation: Newman argues that, whilst Shakespeare's work is not free from the prejudices of his time, the play's fundamental plot and characterisations challenge at least some of the racist and patriarchal discourses of early modern England.

Analysis:

- To support her argument, Newman focusses on the marriage between Desdemona and Othello, which symbolises how society might overcome racism and gender inequality. This is communicated in Othello's description of Desdemona as "my fair warrior" and Desdemona's dedication to her husband.
- However, this glimmer of hope for a better society is extinguished by the plot's overall direction. Having deceived her father, Desdemona is unable to liberate herself from the rumours that she is dishonest, and Othello is forced into the mould of the irrational, violent husband. Their deaths on the marriage bed at the play's denouement symbolise the impossibility of their dream of equality.

Use in essays on… The Tragic Hero; The Tragic Victim; Gender; Race.

Ben Okri (1997) suggests Othello must be seen as,
"the white man's myth of the black man."

Interpretation: Okri argues that Othello is the creation of a white, western imagination and is therefore shaped by history, prejudice, and stereotyping.

Analysis:
- Whilst Othello is presented as noble in Act One Scene Two, the racist language of Act One Scene One ("black ram" and "beast with two backs") sets the tone for the play. It frames the characterisation of Othello within the discourse of inescapable otherness and prejudice.
- Even when Othello is portrayed as heroic and rational in Act One Scenes Two and Three, Shakespeare emphasises his subservience to the senators (he is given permission to speak by the Duke, and addresses his listeners as "my very noble and approved good masters").
- Finally, Othello's descent into madness in the falling action can be seen to confirm, rather than challenge, these stereotypes.

Use in essays on… The Tragic Hero; Race.

Hugh Quarshie (1999) poses the question,
"[I]f a black actor plays Othello does he not risk making racial stereotypes seem legitimate and even true?"

Interpretation: Continuing Okri's line of argument, Quarshie considers the play from an actor's perspective. Quarshie believes that the characterisation of Othello is marked by – and confirms – racist stereotypes.

Analysis:
- In the falling action, we see Othello overtaken by "passion" and falling into an irrational "trance". Although in Act Five Scene One Othello insists that he has been "perplexed in the extreme" by Iago, the image of the black man murdering the white woman on their marriage bed remains. Additionally, the tragic hero is reduced to the cold phrase "the Moor" in the play's final lines, and the play ends with condemnation of "the tragic loading of this bed".
- Yet, Quarshie played Othello in the 2015 RSC production. This play challenged the traditional dynamic as a black actor was cast in the role of Iago, negating continuation of stereotypes around intelligence vs ignorance.

Use in essays on… The Tragic Hero; Race; Rational vs Irrational.

Performance History

Early productions of Othello would have been all-male, all-white casts. However, it is important to note 17th Century London would have had people from many races and ethnicities within it. Cassio's description of Othello as a "great" Captain, or Lodovico's description of the "noble Moor", highlight their ability to recognise Othello's achievements, and early productions would have foregrounded many facets and interpretations of Othello's character, not simply his skin colour.

In the 1820s, Ira Aldridge was the first black professional actor to play Othello; however, his role in an American production ended after pressure from the pro-slave lobby. It took until 1943 for another black actor, Paul Robeson, to play Othello on Broadway, in an historic performance that saw a black man kiss a white woman on stage for the first time in the USA. Jim Crow laws were still in place in much of America at this time; with a black man kissing a white woman on stage, how might audience members react to Iago's statement that "an old black ram is tupping your white ewe"?

Throughout the 19th and 20th century, some productions had actors alternating the roles of Othello and Iago. What could this do to interpretations of identity within the play? Iago's claim "I am not what I am" could be seen in many ways when 24 hours later the actor is playing Othello. Iago states Othello "Hath leap'd into my seat"; what does alternating actors do to interpretations about Iago's motivations?

In 2015, Iqbal Khan's RSC production cast Hugh Quarshie as Othello but also cast a black actor, Lucian Msamati, as Iago. Furthermore, Nadia Albina, a disabled actress, played the Duke of Venice. If one argues casting a black Iago removes the driving force of "racial stereotypes" (Quarshie, 1999) in Iago's motivation, how does this sit alongside G.K Hunter's view earlier (1967)? Also, if a disabled, female Duke arguably dampens both the idea of a prejudice or misogynistic Venice, how does this alter the suggestion Desdemona and Emilia are given 'permission' to speak by a male society?

How to revise effectively.

One mistake people often make is to try to revise EVERYTHING!

This is clearly not possible.

Instead, once you understand the text in detail, a good idea is to pick five or six major themes, and four or five major characters, and revise these in great detail. The same is true when exploring key scenes – you are unlikely to be able to closely analyse every single line, so focus on the *skills* of analysis and interpretation and then be ready for any question, rather than covering the whole text and trying to pre-prepare everything.

If, for example, you revised Iago and Jealousy, you will also have covered a huge amount of material to use in questions about Power, Othello or Appearance and Reality.

It is also sensible to avoid revising quotations in isolation; instead, bring together two or three textual quotations as well as a critical and contextual quotation so that any argument you make is supported and explored in detail.

Finally, make sure material is pertinent to the questions you will be set. By revising the skills of interpretation and analysis you will be able to answer the actual question set in the exam, rather than the one you wanted to come up.

Suggested Revision Activities

A great cover and repeat exercise – Cover the whole page, apart from the quotation at the top. Can you now fill in the four sections without looking – Interpretations, Techniques, Analysis, Use in essays on…?

This also works really well as **a revision activity with a friend** – cover the whole page, apart from the quotation at the top. If you read out the quotation, can they tell you the four sections without looking – Interpretations, Techniques, Analysis, Use in essays on…?

For both activities, could you extend the analysis and interpretation further, or provide an alternative interpretation? Also, can you find another quotation that extends or counters the point you have just made?

Your very own Quotation Bank! Using the same headings and format as The Quotation Bank, find 10 more quotations from throughout the text (select them from many different sections of the text to help develop whole text knowledge) and create your own revision cards.

Essay writing – They aren't always fun, but writing essays is great revision. Devise a practice question and try taking three quotations and writing out a perfect paragraph, making sure you add connectives, technical vocabulary and sophisticated language.

Glossary

Allusion – Referring to something in a sentence without mentioning it explicitly: Iago's Biblical allusion is to Exodus 3:14, in which God reveals his eternal, unchanging goodness in the statement, "I am who I am".

Blank Verse – Lines that do not rhyme but are spoken in regular metre, usually iambic pentameter: blank verse contrasts with Iago's descent into prose in Act One Scene One – the former represents order and rationality, the latter indicates chaos.

Euphemism – An indirect way of expressing something unpleasant: "leap'd into my seat" suggests that Iago believes Othello has had an affair with Emilia.

Imagery – Figurative language that appeals to the senses of the audience: animal imagery exemplifies the racist stereotypes which surround Othello, presenting him as debased, sexualised, and uncivilised.

Imperative – A sentence that gives a command or an order: by using the imperative verb "come", Shakespeare cements Othello's control within the marriage.

Juxtaposition – Two ideas, images or words placed next to each other to create a contrasting effect: the juxtaposition of "immortal"/"bestial" echoes other dichotomies such as judgement/passion, rational/irrational.

Language – The vocabulary chosen to create effect.

Motif – A significant idea, element or symbol repeated throughout the text: throughout the play, the motif of storytelling suggests that the individual who controls the narrative can wield power.

Prose – Normal spoken or written language, instead of verse: in Act Two Scene Three, Shakespeare uses prose and repetition to signal the shift from order to chaos.

Repetition – When a word, phrase or idea is repeated to reinforce it: repetition of "handkerchief" throughout Act Three indicates Othello's obsession with this piece of "ocular proof".

Rhetorical Questions – A persuasive device where the person asking the question already knows the answer: the use of rhetorical questions suggests Lodovico's complete confusion at the situation he finds in Cyprus.